Exmoor's Wild Red Deer

THEIR HISTORY – STATUS –
LIFESTYLE – SENSES

Noel Allen

THE EXMOOR PRESS

© Noel Allen

First Published 1990

By THE EXMOOR PRESS
Dulverton TA22 9EX

BRITISH LIBRARY CATALOGUING IN PUBLICATION DATA
Allen, Noel
    Exmoor's Wild Red Deer
    1. Great Britain. Red Deer
    I. Title
    599.7357

ISBN 0 900131 65 9

Front Cover. The Pride of Exmoor — a large stag.
Back Cover. A stag with hinds.

Printed in Great Britain by Williton Printers, Somerset.

CONTENTS

Illustrations

Colour Photographs: Graham Floyd.
Black and White Photographs: Ray Rendell, except on pages 10 and 11 reproduced by Michael Deering from the originals, page 31 by Tim and Caroline Shipsey and page 33 by Mike Gage.
Line Drawings: Jonathan White.

About the Author

Noel Allen is the founder and Chairman of the Exmoor Natural History Society. He is a well known lecturer and author of several titles published by the Exmoor Press, including THE WATERS OF EXMOOR and (with Caroline Giddens) EXMOOR WILDLIFE, as well as several other works.

A roaring stag during the Autumn rut.

1
Identifying Exmoor's Wild Deer

Three species of wild deer occur within Exmoor National Park: red deer, fallow deer, and roe deer. The red and roe are native to Britain but the fallow is an old introduced species. The usual terms for describing them are:

Species	Male	Female	Young
Red	Stag	Hind	Calf
Fallow	Buck	Doe	Fawn
Roe	Buck	Doe	Kid or Fawn

RED DEER. The largest and most abundant deer in Exmoor, a mature stag standing almost four feet at the shoulder and weighing 300 lbs. Walking or trotting over heather it moves with easy, majestic grace almost as if it knows that it is the pride of Exmoor. During the summer the coat is a rich dark red, turning browner in the autumn and often with a greyish tinge as the winter proceeds. The underparts are lighter, the neck distinctly thicker than the slender neck of the hind, and with a mane from August to December. On the rump the caudal disc around the short but distinct tail is creamish. Only the stag carries antlers and these grow from two permanent round bones on the skull known as pedicles and situated slightly in front of and between the prominent ears. The hind is somewhat smaller, just over three feet at the shoulder, and seldom weighing above 200 lbs. The large, pointed ears are outlined in black, the big eyes a golden colour, and the face growing longer with age. At birth the calf, like most young deer is spotted white, but these fade after a few months to be replaced by a brownish coat.

FALLOW DEER. These are native to some Mediterranean lands and were probably brought to England by the Romans. They have long been the most popular deer kept in parks, and the Exmoor ones are descendants of escapees from former deer parks at Dunster Castle and Nettlecombe Court. In the 1830s John Knight who had purchased the Royal Forest of Exmoor from the Crown enclosed a herd of fallow deer in rough moorland around Simonsbath. By 1850 they had become something of a menace to the farming endeavours of the family and were eliminated by his son Frederic. Within the National Park today they are restricted to woodlands east of the A.396 Dunster to Wheddon Cross road, especially in the Forestry Commission

6

plantations on Croydon Hill, and on Gallox Hill behind Dunster and eastwards on the Brendons towards Monksilver and Stogumber. Here they normally run in small herds of five or six up to 15, but are always very wary being persecuted by foresters and landowners. Fallow deer are not hunted by the staghounds. Over recent years some have been enticed into a deer park at Combe Sydenham.

The fallow is a medium size deer with a number of colour types which is unusual for a wild animal. The normal upper coat is a deep fawn, blotched with large white spots, but many on Exmoor are dark brown, almost black. The buck alone carries antlers, and in an adult these should have bey and trey points with the upper end flattened or palmated. These are shed in early June and the new ones fully grown towards the end of August. Fawns are nearly always born in June and are white-spotted but where both parents are dark the off-spring is likely to be brown. A noticeable feature of all fallow deer is the nine inch long white tail with a broad black line running down its full length and which is constantly on the swish. This alone will distinguish it from any other species of deer on Exmoor. Total numbers on Exmoor are between 300 and 400.

ROE DEER. This is the smallest deer likely to be met within the National Park, an adult standing about two feet at the shoulder and weighing around 60 pounds. Buck and doe are much the same size except the male is rather heavier and carries short antlers forked at the top. The antlers are often very rough or pearled, and unlike other deer are cast in November and regrown by March. The coat is a reddish-brown but greyer during the winter. A most noticeable feature of the roe deer is the clear white caudal (rump) disc, oval in the male and heart-shaped in the female. There is no visible tail but the doe may grow a tuft of white hairs in the winter months which might be mistaken for a small tail. Roe deer live chiefly as a family unit of buck, doe, twin kids of the year, and not in herds. They are almost entirely woodland animals browsing off brambles, shrubs and saplings. It was the new forestry plantations of the 1920s which enabled roe deer to increase and spread over much of southern England after almost dying out in the 19th century. A few reached Exmoor in the 1950s and have since appeared in most large woods and plantations with the greatest numbers in the coastal region. The Exmoor population today is probably around 300.

2
Through the Centuries

Before the coming of the Normans to Britain it seems certain the Saxon kings regularly hunted the red deer of Exmoor. Watchet was an important Saxon port with a royal mint and a number of silver pennies have survived from these early days. The Domesday Survey of 1086 reveals that in the reign of King Edward three Saxon foresters lived at Withypool and their names are given as Dodo, Almor, and Godric. Like the majority of Saxon landowners they were evicted by William the Conqueror and their land given to Robert de Osburville in return for over-seeing the king's Royal Forest of Exmoor. The Anglo-Saxon Chronicle tells how the Conqueror jealously guarded his deer and adds, 'He set apart a vast deer preserve and imposed laws concerning it. Whoever slew a hart or a hind was to be blinded. For he loved the stags as dearly as though he had been their father.'

The special Forest laws imposed by the king prohibited anyone within the Forest boundary possessing bows, arrows, hounds or harriers. Offenders against the 'vert and venison' were to be arrested including knights and priests, and 'no tanner or bleacher of hides shall be resident in his Forests.' All dogs were to be lawed, which involved the cruel practice of cutting off three front toes to hinder them in pursuing game. Forest laws were adminstered through the Swainmote Court which met alternately near Landacre Bridge and in Hawkridge churchyard and dealt with the minor charges of trespass and unlawed dogs. The higher court was the Forest Eyre usually held at Ilchester every three years. This was always a grave and solemn occasion when the king's judges armed with the royal writ dealt with offenders against the deer and damage to their feeding grounds.

At the 1270 Eyre 64 offenders were charged with 'destruction of the Vert of Exmore'. Four of these had died, five listed as 'poor' and let off, and most of the rest were fined 12d. except for William of Blackford, Withypool and seven others who had to pay 2s each. There were 15 cases involving the deer of Exmoor and Hugh of Luccombe was declared to be 'an evil doer to the venison of the Lord King and detained in prison'. Two men from Molland had shot a hind with bows and arrows and hid in the house of John, chaplain of Hawkridge. 'The same chaplain came and is detained in prison'. Later we read 'John the chaplain is pardoned for the sake of the king's soul'.

Though there is no estimate of the number of red deer on Exmoor in these early days the information available suggests they were widely distributed and in fair numbers. For example, in 1257 Reynold de Mohun of Dunster Castle had 'by writ of the Lord King taken four stags and three roebucks from the Forest', and in 1315 Edward II sent an order to the sheriff of Somerset to provide 'of Exmore 20 stags'. These were to be salted down, packed in barrels and kept ready for the king's use.

A major change in the history of Exmoor came in 1508 when Henry VII leased the Forest to Sir Edmund Carew, a Devon knight. The royal grant concluded, 'And of our further grace we grant and give licence to the same Edmund that he himself during his life and all other of our lieges by his authority may freely hunt and course the deer, stags as well as bucks and does. But so nevertheless that on the day of the death of the said Edmund he leave at least 100 deer, stags and bucks and does in the said Forest or Chase of Exmore.'

A pricket (a two-year-old male deer).

Sir Edmund Carew was killed in France in 1513 and was followed as Warden of Exmoor by Sir Thomas Boleyn, father of the ill fated Anne Boleyn. A new lease granted in 1568 to Robert Colshill who owned Porlock Manor stipulated, 'And the said Robert Colshill shall keep, preserve, and feed within the Forest and Chase a suitable and sufficient number of deer for the maintenance of venison called game there'.

In 1590 four men from Withypool were accused by the Warden, Sir John Poyntz of 'killing deer, harbouring deer stealers, and maintaining alehouses within the bounds and liberties of the Forest'. The next year 19 men chiefly from Dulverton and Exford were accused of 'killing and carrying away many red deer out of the Forest of Exmoor'. Poaching of deer continued throughout the 16th and 17th centuries and rarely seems to have stopped and persists to this day though with few serious outbreaks in recent years.

The final two Wardens of Exmoor before its sale early in the 19th century were successive Sir Thomas Aclands who were also Masters of the North Devon Staghounds. When Holnicote their West Somerset house near Selworthy was burned down in 1779 the baronet is reputed to have said, 'I regret the loss of my fine collection of stag heads more than the melting of the family silver'. The second Sir Thomas succeeded in 1785 and over the next eight years killed 101 stags and an unrecorded number of hinds. Some of these heads are still displayed in the stables at Holnicote, now National Trust property. Over this period Parson Boyse of Withypool kept a hunting diary which records that the pack consisted of 23 couples of thoroughbred staghounds. The entry for 31 August, 1789 reads, 'The hounds killed several sheep. Sir Thomas ordered the huntsman to hang himself and the whole pack'.

Lord Graves of Bishops Court, Exeter was Master of Staghounds in 1811, and at the close of the season handed things over to Lord Ebrington, later 4th Earl Fortescue, together with a long letter describing the pack, method of hunting, and the state of the deer. He estimated the red deer as 'about 200 head, perhaps 100 short of what there was in old Sir Thomas Acland's time. We know of ten stags at Haddon and Oakford, six at Bray, one at Satterleigh, besides 20 at Horner and one that frequents Badgworthy covert. All these are warrantable, and for the most part heavy old deer. We killed ten stags in 1811 and 30 hinds.'

In 1818 the Royal Forest was sold and enclosed and this was quickly followed by the enclosure of some of the surrounding commons. Local hunting folk were dismayed and disheartened by the rapid multiplication of fences and walls and in 1825 the big staghounds, the only ones in the country, were sold to a German baron and shipped off to the Continent. Dr. Charles Collyns of Dulverton writing of these days says, 'The deer are being driven

A staghunt in Dulverton in 1818. *(Courtesy of Ms Hilary Binding).*

out by high farming and a denser population from their high fastnesses. Even there the ploughshare creaks and the mattock rings; new fences daily encroach upon the space left to the monarch of the Forest; and perhaps the present generation may witness the death of the last wild deer in Devon and Somerset'.

Fortunately, this well-loved Dulverton doctor proved to be a false prophet regarding the demise of the deer, though for some years after 1830 it was touch and go as to whether they could survive on Exmoor. Poaching and shooting became rife, and during this period deer numbers sank to below one hundred. Attempts were made to safeguard the deer and to re-establish hunting but everything was very spasmodic until 1855 when Fenwick Bisset began his long reign as Master of the newly formed Devon and Somerset Staghounds. Once again definite efforts were made to preserve deer by Frederic Knight in the Brendon coverts, by the Earl of Lovelace who planted 800 acres of conifer cover above Culbone, and by Nicholas Snow at Oare who made a 300 acre deerpark which was kept clear of sheep, cattle and trespassers.

In 1875 Fenwick Bisset built the existing hunt stables and kennels at Exford, and with the rebuilding of the two hotels, the 'White Horse' and the 'Crown', it became the hunting centre of Exmoor. Slowly the number of deer increased and to confirm this success Edward, Prince of Wales came to a meet near Porlock in August 1879, and was up with the hounds when the stag was brought to bay in Badgworthy Water. In his final year as Master in 1881 Fenwick Bisset killed 75 deer and at this time numbers were reckoned to be about 500. By the close of the century Exmoor was described as 'full of deer', and in 1898 the Earl of Lovelace put up a high wire fence to keep deer out of his fields. This was the first deer fence erected on Exmoor. Numbers were now estimated at about 1,500 with the hunt killing 250 a year, and popular meets at this time drawing 400 riders and double as many carriage and foot followers.

Fenwick Bisset, with the Devon and Somerset Staghounds at Badgworthy Water, 1871.
(Engraving from a painting by Samuel Carter).

There was some hunting of deer throughout World War I and also a good deal of shooting which reduced numbers to around 700. They remained much the same up to World War II when large tracts of moorland were taken over by the Army for training. With the return to near normal conditions hunting was again resumed on a regular basis, and with it efforts to increase the deer population mainly by the farming community. By 1980 numbers of red deer within Exmoor National Park had climbed once more to 1,000, and now ten years on to around 1,500.

3
Distribution and Numbers

First of all a brief look at the red deer population in Great Britain today starting with Scotland. Here most are in the northern half, with some on a few off-shore islands and a pocket in the south-west corner of the country. Total numbers in Scotland are reckoned to be about 240,000 with some 40,000 culled annually. In England there are several hundred red deer in the Lake District; a herd in the Forestry Commission conifer forest, Thetford, Norfolk, and a few in the New Forest. The greatest density is in South-West England with about 500 on the Quantocks, 1,500 within Exmoor National Park, and some 400 immediately south of the border towards South Molton and Tiverton. A few wanderers have travelled as far as Dartmoor in recent years where a small resident population is now established.

Numbers in a herd may vary from five or six up to 35 or 40, and there are a few solitary red deer about. Hind herds are more numerous on Exmoor than stag groups. The make-up of a herd is not rigid and a hind group will often contain calves and male deer up to two and three years old or even a mature stag. Few stag herds total more than ten, and a herd of 20 is exceptional on Exmoor.

Hind and mixed herds will be led by a healthy, mature hind eight to ten years old and nearly always with a calf. As leader she will be well acquainted with the local feeding grounds, and with the handy sheltered nooks when gales blow or the clouds open up, for the yearly rainfall on moorland Exmoor varies between 65 and 90 inches. She will also know the safest escape routes when danger threatens, and will lead the herd from the front followed by her calf. Stag herds seem to be less organised but they co-exist peacefully except during the autumn rut. There is practically no friction between herds and on occasions may join up for a while, and when scattered by the Hunt will reform within a few hours on their old territory. They are lovers of the sun and lie out enjoying its warmth whenever possible apart from really hot days when they may seek the shade of nearby trees. Like most animals they normally look for shelter in severe weather and when wet will shake themselves like dogs sending out showers of spray. Red deer are largely creatures of habit, and once the movement of a herd has been worked out it can nearly always be discovered in its everyday haunts.

Exmoor National Park covers 265 square miles or 165,000 acres, two-thirds in Somerset and the balance in Devon. Some 16,000 acres or nearly one-tenth is woodland, much old oak woods perched on the steep sided valleys of Horner and Hawkcombe waters, the Lyn rivers, and bordering the rivers Barle and Exe. The coastal woods from Porlock Weir to Glenthorne and around Woody Bay are just as precipitous.

By preference red deer are animals of the woodland fringe, seeking shelter and safety among the trees, and feeding on nearby open land and fields.

Stags search woodland for fodder when snow covers moorland, heather and grass.

Exmoor has 40,000 acres of moorland, half heather and the rest mainly molinia grass with some deer sedge, cotton grass, rushes and whortleberry. The balance is largely sheep and cattle pasture, with arable in the Porlock Vale and along the coastal belt east of Dunster. More than half of Exmoor is above 1,000 feet, rising to 1,705 feet at Dunkery Beacon, and to 1,600 feet on The Chains where the rivers Barle, Exe, West Lyn and Bray, and numerous waters have their source.

The National Trust are the biggest single landowners with some 20,000 acres including the vital red deer area around Dunkery. The National Park Authority owns 6,000 acres, much of it important oak woodland and grass moor.

On Croydon Hill and Brendon Hill the Forestry Commission has 3,000 acres of conifer plantations which harbour a few red deer, but mostly fallow and a few roe. The League Against Cruel Sports owns land, mainly woodland, in the Exe Valley around Barlinch with good numbers of red deer. Taken altogether, Exmoor with its widespread moors, deep well sheltered wooded valleys and high pasture, provides an ideal habitat for the wild red deer.

Although red deer are able to exploit a wide variety of country the majority on Exmoor prefer to live in three main areas. The most important is the National Trust moorland rising above the 900 acres Horner Woods and stretching for four miles from Robin How, through the Dunkery slopes to Lucott Cross. Close by and nearer the coast is Ley Hill and Porlock Common with the woods of Hawkcombe and Shillets. Between 350 and 400 red deer harbour in this part of Exmoor and account for at least 25% of the total number. Deer in the Dunkery region of Hollowcombe, Allercombe, Sweetworthy, and Bagley are usually in small herds of about 15, but further west around Chetsford Water, on Honeycombe Hill, Embercombe, Great and Little Hill, there are regular herds of 30 and more. Ley Hill has a nice complement of deer, and the Hawkcombe woods are a regular place for a stag herd though numbers have recently been affected by fresh deer fences around adjoining grass fields.

Another red deer stronghold is the Quarme and Exe valleys below Wheddon Cross to Exebridge on the south border of the National Park. Much of this area is wooded where the deer spend most of the daylight hours before venturing forth at dusk to feed in the nearby fields. Deer are more difficult to count among trees but numbers in this rather narrow eight mile stretch are around 250, including several good stag herds. There are deer also in the upper part of the Exe beneath Warren Farm including a few big stags, and below Exford between Lyncombe and Nethercot under Winsford Hill, and on Bye Common.

The Barle valley is well wooded below Withypool with the Danes Brook running into it at Castle Bridge under Hawkridge. Deer are scarce above Landacre Bridge apart from a few near Squallacombe, and the largest numbers in the Barle valley harbour in the woods between Withypool and Dulverton and up the Danes Brook where they spread out on to Anstey and Molland commons. Here again, the red deer population is about 250.

Along the coast there are deer on North Hill, Minehead living in the Selworthy and Bossington woods and in Bramble Combe running down to the sea. Numbers here are at least 70 and things are much the same on Grabbist to the south of the town. Further west there are resident deer in Porlock Parks, Worthy and Culbone woods, and Pitcombe and in Weir woods but many have been shot in some of these places over the past few years.

Glenthorne has its quota of deer, both red and roe, and there are increasing numbers in the Heddon valley and some in Cowley Wood near Parracombe. A little group of stags often spend the summer behind Badgworthy Wood quite unknown to the thousands of visitors who toil up the valley in quest of the Doones. Not many red deer are seen beyond the Simonsbath to Lynton road apart from some wandering stags in the Farley woods, and occasional hinds on The Chains and its valleys. In the eastern section of the National Park the Stowey woods above Timberscombe, Kennisham Hill on the Brendons, Croydon Hill and Pittleigh near Wheddon Cross, all have deer. There are red deer also all along the southern border around Brayford, Heasley Mill and Molland.

A mature stag.

4
The Yearly Round

WINTER — THE LEAN MONTHS. By the onset of winter the red deer have generally settled into stag and hind herds with the calves and some prickets remaining with the hinds. Each of the three major deer areas on Exmoor holds its own herd of 15 to 20 stags plus smaller groups of four or five. There are also some solitary stags which seek out some quiet corner for most of the year. This may be in a small plantation, among a gorse thicket, or an isolated combe where they lie up during the day before setting out to feed at dusk.

A group of stags in winter.

Severe weather rarely comes to Exmoor before the turn of the year and then there may be difficult times for moorland sheep, cattle, and ponies, and the wild red deer. With the threat of snow, and it comes most years to the high land, farm stock is moved down to lower ground, but the deer remain sheltering in the lee of hills, among clumps of hawthorn and gorse, and along woodland edges. Heavy snow quickly buries much of their food but they continue to paw the ground to get at grass, whortleberry, and heather, and search the woods for ivy and holly, and the hedgerows for bramble leaves. Some will descend to lower fields where snow may be absent and grass and root crops available, and a few emboldened by hunger will raid out-lying gardens, allotments, and even cemeteries.

Winter is the hardest time of the year for deer with a general shortage of food, and the big oak woods now leafless, cold, and affording little shelter from the keen winds. These are the lean months, but there is food for the searching, and there is no starvation on Exmoor.

SPRING — CASTING OF ANTLERS. Spring is rarely delayed beyond the end of March and brings with it warmer days and a growing abundance of food. This additional food coincides with the greater need of the deer for now most hinds are carrying calves to be born in mid-summer, and stags are about to renew their antlers, or 'horns' to local folk. This annual casting of antlers is unique to the deer family and does not occur with sheep and cattle. The biggest stags start to drop their antlers towards the end of March and into April, followed by younger stags and prickets up to the middle of May. It is brought about by the drying up of the blood supply at the base of the antler until the connection with the pedicle becomes dead and brittle. Then a jump or a sudden jolt will shake them off, though it is rare for both antlers to fall off together. Usually there is a delay of a day or so before the second is cast. Searching for dropped antlers is an Exmoor pastime and some who follow it vigorously find a dozen in a season. The more casual walker on Exmoor may also stumble across one, and every year there are a few fortunate finders who carry an antler home in triumph.

It is an old saying that red deer antlers grow in pace with the bracken on the hills, and this is roughly correct. Once the old antlers have been cast the new ones immediately start to develop from the pedicles and for the next three months will have a rubber-like appearance covered by a thick skin known as velvet which protects the blood vessels and nerves. By early August the new growth will be complete and the antler hardens into solid bone and the velvet rubbed off on a shrub or young conifer. A good antler will consist of a strong main beam, and branching from it and nearest the head the brow point, a bey point in the middle, and a trey point above. The top end of the main beam also divides into short points, and a seven year old stag should have brow, bey and trey points, and three short points at the top, and will be described on Exmoor as a stag with 'All his rights and three atop'. A handful of stags never grow antlers, nott stags they are called, but they still carry the greater bulk and thicker necks of normal male deer. The 'switch head', where a long main beam carries only the two brow points, also occurs. More rare are one horned stags, or those with deformed heads as a pair of antlers are termed. Deformity may be congenital, but more often due to damage in the growing antler when it is soft and in velvet. In the latter case it will right itself the following year.

It is difficult to lay down hard and fast rules about antler development. Good or poor heads no doubt depend on breeding and on the available calcium and phosphorous in the food supply. Given satisfactory conditions growth of a head should be:

1st year of life ... Pedicles only showing.
2nd year of life ... Short uprights, slightly longer than ears.
3rd year of life ... Lengthening of uprights and small brow point.
4th year of life ... Generally a bigger antler, now with brow and trey points. Possibly small two atop.
5th year of life ... Good medium antler, growth of bey point and two atop.
6th year of life ... Thickening of main beam, lengthening of all points.
7th year of life ... Now three atop and a good large antler.

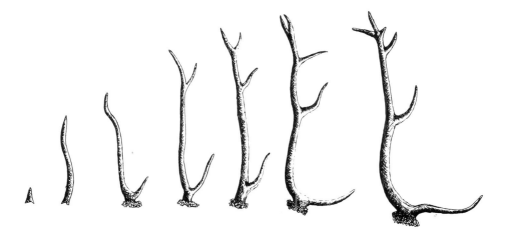

Development of antlers over seven years.

Some additional points atop may be added over the next three years with the whole antler becoming heavier and massive in appearance. An acceptable point is any projection on which a ring can be hung. A large pair of antlers weigh between ten and twelve pounds.

As it gets older a stag's forehead tends to broaden and a hind's face to lengthen. In both cases the head is carried lower when walking, and the muzzle turns greyer. Between tne ages of seven to ten a stag is in his prime, but at twelve the antlers begin to deteriorate or 'go back' when the points atop tend to merge and flatten and the main beam becomes thinner. At fifteen a red deer is old but few survive beyoi.J this age on Exmoor where hunting weeds out the sick and feeble.

A stag in velvet.

SUMMER — BIRTH OF CALVES. June is the month when most red deer calves are born on Exmoor, with a few early ones at the end of May, and some late ones in July. A few August births have also been recorded in recent years. Hunting red deer is halted for much of this time so the young are born in quiet days. As the birth date approaches individual hinds break away from the herds to retire to a handy thicket or a patch of bracken in a side combe. Some young are born along woodland edges, amid leggy heather and whortleberry, and more rarely among rushes on open moorland. The gestation period is about eight months, and hinds invariably have only one calf with a birth weight of between 15 and 20 lbs. The first calf is born when the mother is two to four years old.

A red deer calf.

The new-born calf is dropped among the vegetation and lies concealed for a while well camouflaged in its white dappled russet coat. Within an hour it is able to stand to take a feed from the mother and perhaps make an attempt to nibble at any young shoots within reach.

Over the next week the calf spends much of its time crouching in the undergrowth its mother feeding some distance away but returning every three or four hours for her off-spring to suckle. Concealment is the calf's best protection from foxes and dogs in these early days and the hind will give a barking warning should any danger approach.

At four days old a calf is strong and active enough to outpace a man, and by a week to ten days is able to run with its mother. Most soon join up with the herd again although a few hinds seem to live very much alone with their calf and often with the calf of the previous year. Young deer never stray far from their mothers and follow them closely as they wander over the feeding grounds. When they sit down to cud a calf will shelter alongside its mother. Should they become separated and feel in danger the calf will bleat like a goat. All deer are rather sober creatures but young stags will have antler pushing contests and calves will join up to gambol among the hinds.

Towards the end of the summer the white spots on the young fade away but up until their second birthday they can always be told by their smaller size. It is important that any calf found lying out on its own should be left strictly alone. Its chances of survival are minimal if taken away in any attempt to rear it. The mother knows where it is and will come back to feed it in due time.

AUTUMN — THE RUT OR MATING MONTHS. As the end of September approaches deer are in fine condition from the lush feeding of the summer months and the early autumn harvest of acorns and sweet chestnuts. Now their russet coats appear at the very best and the antlers of the stags clean of velvet gleam in the slanting sun as they lie contented among the warm heather. Soon, however, there will be a stirring among the herds for the months of October and November are days of the rut or mating time when stags move out in search of the hinds. Those from Hawkcombe and Porlock Parks to Great and Little Hill above Chetsford Water, the Horner stags up on to Ley Hill and the combes of the Dunkery slopes, and the few harbouring in Badgworthy and Weir woods to Mill Hill, and some will travel further to find the hinds on North Hill, Minehead and Alcombe Common. Those in the Exe, Barle and Danesbrook valleys have not so far to go but may face competition from stags coming out of woods around Brayford, Heasley Mill and Molland.

The rut begins with a general mingling of stags among the hinds and calves. After a few days the largest and most powerful stags will rush at the other male deer in the group in an attempt to drive them away from the hinds. This show of superiority is often only partially successful and some of the defeated stags will generally manage to make off with a few hinds leaving ten or a dozen with the master stag. Young stags unable to collect hinds at the start of the rut will continue to hang around the outskirts of a herd making sallies among the hinds in an endeavour to isolate one or two for themselves. Occasionally two big stags of near equal size will battle for the mastery of a group of hinds. Then a real battle ensues lasting up to half-an-hour as they rush at one another with a great clash of antlers, battling for the advantage of any higher slope in an attempt to throw the rival to the ground. A particularly fierce contest will see blood flowing freely from head and neck wounds until one admits defeat and reluctantly slinks away. It does happen that while these fights are going on a third stag slips in and makes off with the hinds.

Throughout the six or so weeks of the rut there is a great roaring among the stags, challenge and counter-challenge echoes through the woods and across the combes. At this time the hinds will continue to browse quietly, chevied by the stags should they wander too far away. When possible the stags try to rest in the daytime and rarely feed, but usually have to rouse themselves up from time to time to drive off a young interloper. By mid-November the rut begins to die down, the biggest stags relax their guard and the smaller ones make the most of the opportunities to get among the hinds. By the start of December there is a general mixing of the herds again but by the end of the year most of the stags move away to regroup in their own herds.

Overleaf: stag and hinds at rutting time.

5
Food and Feeding

Red deer are herbivores, browsers rather than grazers, and feed off a wide variety of shrubs, saplings, plants, grasses and fruits. On the open moor much of their regular diet consists of young heather and whortleberry shoots, grass and sedges, and sometimes bracken shoots are eaten in the spring. On the whole they are selective feeders, moving slowly forward as they carefully collect each bite. The food intake of hill deer has been found to consist of 40% heather and whortleberry; 15% sedges; 20% moss and 25% grass. There is little evidence that heather is over grazed on Exmoor or of over-stocking of deer. The three species of deer within the National Park total at the most 2,500 which gives one to 66 acres. In Scotland 240,000 deer roam over seven million acres with a ratio of about one deer to 30 acres.

Away from the moors bramble leaves and grass are great favourites with the deer together with any root crops they can get at. They are also fond of potatoes, apples, growing and eared corn, and wild fruits will include acorns, crab apples, beech mast and some fungi. Deer and sheep show little hostility to one another and feed amicably over the same heather or grass. It is reckoned that two deer will eat as much as three sheep.

Deer have eight incisors in the lower jaw; these are the front cutting teeth which bite against a hard gum pad and not against other teeth as in dogs, horses and humans. No doubt this arrangement prevents some wear on the cutting teeth which are vital to the deer's suvival for without them it would be difficult for the animal to gather sufficient food. On both sides of the lower and upper jaw there are the grinding teeth made up of three molars and three premolars. So a deer with a full set has a total of 32 teeth. With cutting teeth only in the lower jaw it is usual for vegetation to be half-bitten through and then torn away leaving a characteristic red deer mark.

All deer are ruminants and spend two or three hours browsing and passing the food with very little chewing into a separate compartment of the stomach. Then they find a quiet spot to lie down and cud. Here the food is brought back to the mouth in small balls, thoroughly chewed, swallowed for the second time into the main digestive part of the stomach. Deer have a natural drop of appetite during the winter when their food requirements are reduced to almost half, but this is followed by months of greatest need when calves are near to being born, and stags growing new antlers. Then it is reckoned a hind will gather 15 lbs. of fresh vegetation and a big male 20 lbs. each day.

There is always the problem of deer getting among crops and newly planted woodland in search of food, and the recommended height for a deer fence is a minimum of six feet. However, there are deer who will easily clear seven feet, and hinds will often try to squeeze under a wire fence rather than make the jump. Sometimes the slope of the ground will permit deer to get into young woodland where a lot of damage can be done, but where it is not easy for them to get out. A solution to this problem could be a deer-leap. This consists of providing a broad sloping ramp of soil up to the height of the fence but with a sheer drop of some five feet on the escape side. Another solution is to provide more attractive feeding outside of a sensitive area. This, of course, can be time consuming and expensive, but it is an alternative to shooting where this is undesirable. Many farmers tie plastic bags around their fields but this will normally only deter deer for a while unless the bags are regularly moved around.

6
Deer and Humans

THEIR SENSES — SIGHT, HEARING, SMELL. Deer are well equipped for survival in the wild and with the passing of all our large carnivores (the last wolf on the mainland of Great Britain was killed in Morayshire, Scotland, in 1743) man alone is the chief source of danger. Their sight is obviously very good for their eyes are large and bright and can spot a walker at least half-a-mile off. The rule is, if they can be seen, they can certainly see anyone standing in the open. The ears are big, erect and turn easily to catch any sound, but noise alone does not unduly alarm them. At 50 yards they will hear the crack of a twig or the click of a camera shutter. This will cause them to look up but rarely to move off. Perhaps their keenest sense is that of smell and with a moderate up-wind they can detect humans a mile away. When sight and sound are confirmed by smell they are quickly on their guard and may move away.

Above: a red deer hind.
Opposite: a hind and calf.

SIGNS — SLOTS, DROPPINGS, HAIR, WALLOWS, RACKS AND TRACKS. The most abundant sign that deer are about are the footprints or slots as they are called. Those of a mature stag are about three inches long and two inches across and register on soft ground as a single print with a raised central line, but when running it shows as two separate halves, the front ends much wider apart and more pointed. Hind slots are rather smaller and calves half the size.

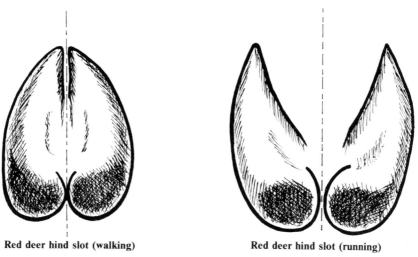

Red deer hind slot (walking)   **Red deer hind slot (running)**

Adult deer droppings are about three-quarters of an inch long, elliptical and pointed at one end, black in colour and left in groups. During the rut stag droppings are more like miniature cowpats.

During the late spring when the winter coats are moulted tufts of grey-brown hair can be seen in many cudding and sheltering places. Hair is often left on barbed wire fences which deer have jumped.

Wet, muddy wallows the size of a deer's body are widely scattered over the moor at spring-heads and in boggy patches often under willow and hawthorn bushes. Lower down they can be found by woodland streams and amid thickets. Both stags and hinds use them in hot summer months when flies are troublesome, and by the stags in the rut. They are easily told by the smooth, hair-matted sides of the mud wallow, and by slots in the adjoining ground.

When unmolested and unhurried deer travel along regular tracks when moving out from shelter and into their feeding areas. Where this passes through hedges and thickets or across woodland rides a clear gap or rack is made in the undergrowth. Well worn tracks are made over the steepest banks.

HUNTING AND CULLING. Bearing in mind the damage deer can do to plantations and on agricultural land and the limit to the tolerance of farmers, the red deer of Exmoor have probably today now reached maximum acceptable numbers. True, deer are rather thin on the ground in the eastern half of the National Park but they are really quite abundant in their preferred haunts. Near the end of the year the average hind herd will include 25% calves, and the annual natural population increase is between 300 and 400. So some culling is essential, and the traditional way in the West Country is by hunting with hounds. When the hunted deer is brought to bay it is then shot at close quarters. Hunting is opposed nationwide by the League Against Cruel Sports who own deer sanctuaries on Exmoor, and by a few groups of local residents. The pros and cons are a continual subject in the letter columns of the local press, much of it ill-informed. The one important question is, 'What is best for the deer', and both sides seem to agree that some culling is essential. Hunting in many ways would seem to be the natural way, for deer were certainly hunted by wolves in the old days, and still are by leopards and lions in Africa. The other method is, of course, shooting.

**A meet of the Devon and Somerset Staghounds.
Pitcombe Head, October 1988.**

WATCHING DEER. (See also the section on Senses at the start of this chapter.) Deer are not really difficult to find and watch but they do fade remarkably well into the brown colours of the moorland landscape and it often needs an experienced eye to spot them. They are alert animals and to get within 50 yards of them a careful down-wind (wind blowing from deer to stalker) approach is necessary. A browsing or cudding herd will always have a few old experienced hinds constantly looking-up and on the watch for signs of danger. Too hurried an approach or the sudden disappearance of the stalker into a hollow is sure to put them on their guard. Sometimes deer may be surprised in woodland or in a combe bottom, and then it is best to remain perfectly still and there is a good chance that after a long stare they will settle down again.

A stag and hind at Selworthy.

Stags retreating through a hedge.

Red deer will often stand and watch walkers or riders on well-used paths but will soon retreat if any attempt is made to get nearer to them. So the advice is, remain on the path where the deer are used to seeing walkers, and often a good view can be obtained with binoculars (probably 8 x 40 are the best) and a satisfactory picture obtained using tele-photo lens of 300 mm upwards.

The secret in getting close to deer is to spot them before they spot you. Deer feeding on open moorland can often be detected a mile or more away. Then if you know the country well it may be possible to plan an approach route which will keep you out of their direct sight until the last moment. This may be done through a combe, along a wall or hedge, behind a screen of bushes, or as a last resort by crawling through the heather. Deer in wooded parts like the Barle and Exe valleys can often be watched at dusk when they come out to get among the grass and crops of the neighbouring fields. After foraging through the night they generally remain in the open until disturbed or the time has come to cud. So an early morning watch can also be rewarding. The true lover of the deer will watch and admire, noting their habits and instincts which have enabled them to survive on Exmoor through many centuries, but will never unduly disturb them.

7
Surviving the Future

HOPES AND FEARS. Red deer have roamed the woods and moors of Exmoor for hundreds of years, almost certainly long before the days of recorded history. There have been years of crisis when their survival hung in the balance, especially in the first half of the 19th century with the enclosure of the Royal Forest and many surrounding commons. With the support and protection from some local enthusiasts the deer survived and today cope well with the bigger numbers of stock and walkers wandering over their traditional feeding grounds. An important factor in their favour has been the increase of woodland within the Exmoor National Park over the past 150 years from about 6,000 acres to 16,000 acres today affording them greater cover, shelter, and food. Some of the best red deer country is owned by the National Trust and the National Park Authority and both are sympathetic to the survival of the red deer.

The problem today and perhaps casting a shadow over the future is the indiscriminate shooting of deer for venison. Invariably the biggest and best deer are shot with little concern for the maintenance of a balanced population. The same is true of most culling undertaken when deer are damaging crops and trees. The ratio of male to female calves at birth is on a 1:1 basis which is nature's way of indicating the proper balance. There are however far more hinds on Exmoor than male deer and the ratio is more like 4:1.

On the other hand an indiscriminate preservation of the red deer would be disastrous for this would mean an annual population increase of some 25% and rapid over-stocking. This in turn would lead to shortage of food, weaker deer succumbing to disease and more poaching with its attendant cruelty. At present uncontrolled shooting results in an imbalance of the herds as regards both sex and age. In brief, more prime stags need to survive to maintain a strong, healthy and vigorous population. With this, and with much of their habitat in 'safe hands', the future of the red deer of Exmoor can be assured. Here they can live a full and satisfying life, and give us the delight of watching them contented and free.

A lead of stags.

Bibliography

Collyns, C. P. — *Notes on the Chase of the Wild Red Deer.* Lawrence and Bullen, 1862. The first printed account of Exmoor's red deer, written by a Dulverton doctor.

Fortescue, J. W. — *Records of Stag-Hunting on Exmoor.* Chapman and Hall, 1887. This up-dates Dr. Collyns's work and was followed by similar books by Evered (1902) and Hamilton (1907).

MacDermot, E. T. — *The Devon and Somerset Staghounds, 1907-1936.* Collins, 1936. With fine coloured plates by Lionel Edwards.

Lloyd, E. R. — *The Wild Red Deer of Exmoor.* Exmoor Press, 1970 and 1975. An authorative work by a local expert, but now out of print.

Allen N. and Giddens C. — *Exmoor Wildlife.* Exmoor Press, 1989. An up-to-date and general account of Exmoor's fauna and flora.